Norma Smoker
and
Rachel Smoker Cox

*une de sus, de la
Suungeu.
♡ Braua*

got kids?
take notes

A quick reference guide to raising children

*For Monica,

my sweet friend.

I pray that God is

always with you and

your baby.*

Love, Diana M.

Blackstone Media Group
PO Box 935148
Fort Lauderdale, FL 33093
bmgcreative.com

First Edition: April 2013

Contents

Acknowledgments

There are several special people I would like to thank for their encouragement and help with this booklet of parenting notes:

Annie Shyne, who has told me to write a book for the past fifteen years and never gave up on me. Annie is a mother of three wonderful children: Nicolas, Gaby, and Alexander. She teaches Latin and Spanish, and has offered to translate this booklet in Spanish!

Liza Smoker, our first born, who called me from her dorm room during her first semester in college and said, "Mom, you have to write your book! Some of these girls have no clue how to handle their newfound freedom!" Liza always believed I should write a book on parenting.

Rachel Smoker Cox, our second born, for the hours she spent alongside me, reading and editing the first drafts of this booklet. As you can imagine, there were many corrections since French is my native language. I am also grateful she did not delete all the stories about her, which I'm sure will make you smile.

Holly Carroll, with whom I have a long history. We met when our girls were in second grade. She has designed the marketing materials for events we helped produce over the years, including the format of this book and its cover.

Shelley Marcenko Arminio, for the cover photo. She is a talented photographer and her photo of Wyatt, our friends' son, truly captures the spirit of childhood we were looking for. Look for more photos from Shelley on her website: monkeyfacephoto.com.

Dionysia "Dee" Moustakas, our editor, whom I had the pleasure of meeting shortly before beginning my search for a professional editor. She is an amazing woman, easy to work with, and has been a God-send to this project.

Jean Gillen, who graciously invited me to co-host her radio program in 1997 which gave me the opportunity to interview hundreds of speakers and authors. When Jean moved to Malaysia, she encouraged the radio station to keep me as its host.

All the men and women who have supported and encouraged me during this process.

Edward Smoker, my husband since 1980 for his support, encouragement, and for giving me complete freedom to follow my passion. He is a wonderful father with the greatest patience and a gentle spirit. I am proud to be his wife and admire his success in both his work and his life.

Most important, God, for His inspiration and guidance.

Introduction

When my daughter, Rachel, was five, I was the leader of a mothers' group called "HOME": Helping Our Mothers Excel. One of my favorite memories was watching Rachel climb up the ladder of her bunk bed one night, whispering under her breath, "I don't know why *you're* the leader of Helping Our Mothers Excel!" I leaned at the doorway of her room thinking, "I don't know either."

Most of us have issues from our childhood. We might have personality traits we would rather live without; and it would help if we could instantly deprogram our minds and lose the baggage we are carrying. However, this journey must often simultaneously happen while we are learning to become parents ourselves.

Is there a perfect, universal method to raising children? No. Because no parents are perfect and all families are different.

What you are about to read is an organization of short, concise notes with word pictures and stories that capture lessons on parenting I have accumulated over a period of thirty years. Some are notes from experts in the field of family living gathered while hosting a radio program. During those seven years, I read a book a week for each author, doctor, psychologist, or specialist whom I had the opportunity to interview. Others are notes compiled from my experiences raising our daughters while working seventeen years with various family outreaches.

You will find "Bottom Line" notations at the end of each Note. I created this format recalling an astute executive I met while working on special events who never wasted time. He would start every meeting with these two words: **Bottom Line.**

Just for fun, I googled "How to write an instructional manual." Most articles suggested starting at square one: Assume the audience has zero knowledge of the subject matter. If your children are older, you will relate to the notes that are most familiar to you. If you know any new parents, you might want to share this booklet with them. It is meant to be a quick study of what to expect.

Most websites also encouraged avoiding information overload and sticking only with what recipients need to know. In other words, use only as many words as necessary. I was tempted to elaborate and add research, statistics, articles, and quotes, but that would defeat the purpose and objective of this project.

I hope you enjoy reading it as much as I enjoyed writing it. It is indeed a labor of love for all the families out there. While it is impossible to help all the children of the world, my mission is to help parents as they raise their little ones.

Note 1

The Cadillac & the Mack Truck

Every child has his or her own personality. Some are easy to bring up. They're like driving a brand-new Cadillac on cruise control on a straight, freshly paved highway. Others are like riding an old Mack truck shifting 14 gears while climbing up a winding and bumpy dirt road. We had one of each.

Whenever I share this analogy with people who know our daughters, they assume Rachel, our second born, is the Mack truck.

Rachel is the creative, free-spirited artist—the adventurous one in our family. After graduating college Magna Cum Laude, she moved on her own to Europe with the little money she had earned working summers and weekends. She lived and worked in London, Ireland, and then

Australia. She took her time exploring in Rome, Florence, Venice, Milan, Scotland, Paris, and Wales. She went skydiving, hang gliding off cliffs, and scuba diving on the Great Barrier Reef—all by the age of 25. Now, she is following her dreams in theater, working as a teacher, actor, director, writer, and stage manager.

So, was it my adventurous, creative child who was the Mack truck? Nope! It was Liza, the lawyer. For Liza, it took considerably more effort to channel her energy throughout her childhood. This does not mean she was a problem child; she just had to do things her own way and we had to learn to be more patient. However, what seemed at the time to be stubbornness, or willfulness, later manifested as a strong sense of self and an aptitude for leadership. In fact, by the time Liza was in her first year of law school, she already had worked for three months at the White House in the President's Council Office.

"My goal was to help them channel their energy and use it to their greatest potential."

One day Liza gave me an unexpected compliment that warmed my heart. While I was helping her get ready for her prom, she proclaimed, "Mom, you're the mother you always wanted to have!"

Both girls were an adventure to bring up and both are the loves of my life. Of all the accomplishments I have achieved or the accolades I have received, there is nothing I cherish more than being their mother.

When I taught elementary school, I must confess I enjoyed the students who challenged me the most. Maybe it was because I saw a little bit of myself in them. That is why I chose to focus on their talents, their possibilities, and their strengths. I certainly was not going to label them as disruptive or argumentative. My goal was to help them channel their energy and use it to their greatest potential. That said, I imagine there are students of mine who might say I was not always that understanding. I am sure that would be true, as it is for all teachers and parents at one time or another.

BOTTOM LINE Whether you have a child who drives like a Cadillac or a Mack truck, enjoy the ride. It does not necessarily mean one turns out better than the other. It only means the journey is different. In the case of a Mack Truck child, parents may need to be more patient, and take a step back before reacting.

Note 2

The Pot and the Bottle

A great place to start our thinking process when we first become parents is to keep this perspective in mind: It is not simply about raising children; it's about bringing them up to become wise, independent, self-confident, happy, and responsible adults.

All research agrees that a child's first three years are the most formative; however, the learning period extends through the age of ten. This is the critical season when parents should give it their all by encouraging, teaching, praising, and nurturing these precious lives while providing for their physical and emotional needs.

When children are young, their minds are wide open. They absorb everything they see and hear like sponges. They're

like large pots with wide openings like the one above. Every word you say becomes a seed planted in their minds. This is the time to wake up their sense of learning and, most important, to nurture their self-esteem.

By the time children reach their preteens, their minds are more like the narrow opening of a bottle. They do not receive and accept as much, or as easily, as they did the first ten years of their lives.

Remember, you only get one shot at it!

 BOTTOM LINE — From the moment your child is born, start pouring your knowledge, values, and virtues into his or her life. Equip your child to become a healthy, educated, and content adult.

Messy Children

I am a neat freak. There, I said it. I do not handle messes very well. In fact, if I came to your home, I would probably start rearranging the piles of paper on your kitchen counter or folding your laundry as we talked. So of course, I had a messy child: Rachel.

Rachel was too busy having fun to put things away. She was like a wind-up doll that would crank up as you lifted her out of her crib in the morning. Her two legs would start pumping in midair, and she would walk around the house all day, carrying everything from one room to another. At night, I'd pick up that tiny doll with her legs still walking on air and set her down down in the crib. Only then, would Rachel finally stop and lie down to sleep.

It was overwhelming and frustrating to gather everything off the floors all day long. When Rachel became old enough, I would fuss at her to put her things back in the toy bins, return her artwork to the art box, or place clothes in her dress-up trunk.

I didn't want to argue with her, injure her self-esteem, or stifle her creativity, but I also didn't want to pick up after her for the next ten years. So, I came up with a plan that would be a "win-win" for both of us. "Rachel, I'm going to make a deal with you. From now on, you can have a messy bedroom, and mommy cannot complain about it anymore. Your part of the deal is you may not leave your things on the floor of the living room, in the kitchen, or anywhere else in the house."

...I came up with a plan that would be a "win-win" for both of us.

From that point on, when I saw something of Rachel's anywhere other than her room, I would simply say, "Your toy needs to go in your room, Rachel. Remember our deal!" She would retrieve it and quickly put it in her room. By the end of the day, I would find myself tiptoeing around all the stuff in her bedroom, but the rest of the house was neat as a pin. I still can see her smiling face nodding at me when I would enter her room and say, "Aren't you relieved mommy isn't allowed to scream at you over the mess in your room anymore?"

In the beginning, I would go into her room before bedtime to show her how to put her toys away. It was a slow learning process, but well worth the effort.

As she got older, her room was often messy, but she always kept our bargain and kept the rest of the house clean. She knew how to clean it up when she wanted to, or when I would ask her to do it as a favor. Now that she has a home of her own, I secretly smile when I see her constantly trying to keep her home organized and clean.

BOTTOM LINE

Instead of being a grouch, come up with a plan that makes life easier for you and your family. That's what successful businesses do, and you are running the most important company of your life. Rules and mutual respect for other family members help make your home more peaceful, perhaps even a sanctuary everyone looks forward to returning to. Spend time discussing each step of the plan until it is clear to everyone. Once complete, sit back, and admire a job well done while praising your children's hard work and effort.

Note 4

A Mother's Voice, the Power Within

The girls have told me that when they are about to make a decision, they often hear my voice in their heads telling them what I think. Fortunately, they added that it helps them make wise choices.

I was a "talking head" in the lives of my daughters. It became comical as they got older. They would interrupt me with, "Yes, Mom, we know!" However, I believe there are things that are worth repeating again and again.

I cannot count the times when moms, who heard me speak on parenting, would tell me that they loved the story about how I talked to the girls while driving in the van. Just last Sunday, a beautiful young mom, who works as a radio station manager, told me she heard me years ago and that is the story she recalled.

When we were in the car, I would take the opportunity to talk to the girls, sometimes "ad nauseam." I would be driving and would say something like, "Do you see this guy on the corner? He has a paper bag wrapped around a can of beer. You don't want to go out with a guy like that. He drinks beer in the middle of the day, and he hides the fact that he is drinking. You can't be hanging around street corners drinking, doing nothing and expect to make a life."

When we would see young women dressed a little too off-colored, I would compare them to others who were tastefully dressed and who moved with style and grace. They came to understand the difference between the classy look, and the "not-so-tasteful look."

Whenever I had the chance, I would give a life lesson from what we would encounter throughout our day.

BOTTOM LINE Don't worry about talking to your children too much. Every lesson "heard" might be the one they recall at the moment it matters most.

Everyone Needs a Coach

Both our daughters undoubtedly knew we were not only their parents but also their "life coaches" ready to equip them to become the very best they could be.

Liza shared that she often visualized herself and Rachel wearing oversized football helmets and jerseys with large shoulder pads while waiting for the carpool in the morning. "My mom was like a football coach, banging on our shoulder pads, kissing the top of our helmets, telling us we were the best kids in the world and that great things were out there for us because we were so awesome."

That is the way she felt we raised her. Well...maybe not all of the time. Of course, I had my moments, and I am sure she can tell you about those, too.

Another year, Liza and her friend were auditioning for a dance number for a show, and I was helping run the music for the instructors. After the audition, I walked by Liza and her friend and whispered close to their ears, "You two were the best!" Liza turned to her friend and said, "See! That's how my mom raised us. She would always tell us we were the best. Now that we're older, we know better, we're not always the best." I quickly interrupted my now "adult" child and said, "Would you have preferred that I said, 'Ehh! You were all right.'?" I am glad she had that to complain about.

BOTTOM LINE Coaches help their team members develop skills by giving them the training they need. They instill confidence in their players through encouragement and support. In the same way, parents need to help boost their child's self-esteem to thrust them towards an accomplished life.

Note 6

Unconditional Love

One evening, Rachel was in the bathroom playing with the water in the sink as she loved to do. There was water all over the floor, and she was on her tippy toes playing with her toys. I came in as she was reaching in to get another toy, and she looked up at me. For a quick instant, I saw a look of worry in her eyes, because she knew she was in trouble with mama. I then said to her, "Rachel, you made a big mess, but I still love you!" Her facial expression relaxed and turned into a big smile. It took so little, yet the message came through.

It was not long after that Rachel began affirming it for herself. As I was scolding her later that week, this sweet toddler clasped her tiny hands together as she stuttered, "But, but mommy, you still love me?" She made my heart melt, as she often did. I got on my knees, took her in my arms and said, "You know it! I will always, always love you, no matter what. No matter how big the mess, no matter what you do, I will always, always love you."

There was another story she loved to hear that reaffirmed my endless love for her, and she would ask me to tell it to her over and over when I tucked her into bed. It went like this, "Rachel, if God had taken me to heaven and asked me to choose from a long line of little girls, I would have picked YOU!" She just loved that story.

BOTTOM LINE

Don't be afraid to triple dose your children with unconditional love. Make it a habit to give them approval every chance you get to nudge them gently in the right direction. There is nothing more valuable for a child's self-worth than the approval and unyielding love of his or her parents.

Name Calling vs. Positive Prophecy

Liza, our first-born, was a baby who would sit calmly in a restaurant eating, looking around, smiling to people watching her, and keep herself entertained through the duration of any meal. Our second-born, Rachel, was more of an "eat and run" kind of gal.

She was not even a year old and a family member kidded that Rachel was going to be my "troublemaker." Of course, the "mama bear" in me rose to the surface to ruthlessly defend my child, but instead out of my mouth came, "Rachel is my happy child." And she became just that. She was always singing and giggling as she pranced about the house dressed up in different costumes. You could always hear her contagious belly laugh echoing across the halls, and it would make us smile. The best news: She is still that way today.

While Rachel was travelling the world, a friend of ours asked me how my "wild" child was doing. I scowled at him and said, "I did not have the opportunity to travel to Europe until I was 55 years old. She, on the other hand, is travelling while she has no ties and is learning to live her life to the fullest. I admire her for her tenacity and courage."

 A book that speaks well on the subject of prophecy is Laurie Beth Jones' *The Path: Creating Your Mission Statement for Work and for Life*. It is by far one of my favorite books, and one I frequently give to others.

BOTTOM LINE

Sometimes your words speak prophecy over your children. Be sure to use positive language and avoid damaging their spirit through criticism.

Perseverance

Will Smith is one of my favorite actors.

I stumbled upon a YouTube video that had a series of video clips of different interviews with him. It truly gives you a peek into his soul and the impact his family's upbringing had on his character. It is illuminated in many of his movies, such as: *Seven Pounds, The Pursuit of Happyness*, and *Men in Black III*.

Here is a sample of the quotes from Will Smith included in the video:

> "I have a great time in my life and I want to share it. I love living. I think that's infectious. It's something that you can't fake."

"Greatness is something that truly exists in all of us. It's very simple: This is what I believe, and I'm willing to die for it; **period**. It's that simple."

"I know who I am. I know what I believe. And that's all I need to know."

"We didn't grow up with the sense that where we were is where we were going to be. We grew up with the sense that where we were almost didn't matter because we were becoming something greater."

"Talents you have naturally. Skills are only developed by hours and hours and hours on your craft. Where I excel is ridiculously, sickening work ethics!"

Smith shares in this video that, when he was young, his father tore down the brick wall in front of his business and told him and his younger brother to rebuild it. Will was twelve years old and his brother was nine. They told their dad the job was impossible. It took them a year and a half, but they did it. His father told them, "Now don't ever tell me there's something you can't do."

He then explained how this relates to life, "You don't start up to build a wall. What you do is you start by laying one brick as perfectly as the brick can be laid. You do that every single day and soon you have a wall."

On the red carpet at one of the award shows, Will shared this about his grandmother: "It's an idea my grandmother always had, that if you were going to be here, there's a necessity to make a difference. She always instilled the spiritual responsibility that you have to make every group you make contact with better." He continued, "I want to do good; I want the world to be better because I was here."

Finally, the last of my favorite quotes from one of his interviews:

"If you're not making someone else's life better then you're wasting your time."

"There is no reason to have a plan B, because it distracts you from plan A."

That is powerful stuff. I could not have said it better. Great words of wisdom, Will Smith!

I love where he says that where he excels is in "ridiculously, sickening work ethics!" If there is one virtue parents should emphasize when teaching their children (one I believe is neglected in

We are not talking about teaching our children to be the best employee at a job, we are teaching them to strive for excellence in all they attempt to accomplish.

this age of instant gratification), it is work ethics. We are not talking about teaching our children to be the best employee at a job, we are teaching them to strive for excellence in all they attempt to accomplish whether in school, sports, arts, etc.

We'll talk more about the virtue of work ethics later in the book, because it promotes so many benefits in character, relationships, and self-confidence. Stay tuned.

BOTTOM LINE

High expectations accompanied by lots of encouragement will inspire your children to aim higher. There's absolutely nothing wrong with that. It helps them become that much more competent and successful at everything they attempt. Encourage them to have as many experiences as they can at each stage of their growth.

Note 9

Etiquette

An easy place to start teaching your children to succeed is in the area of manners and etiquette.

At a very young age, both girls knew to hold out their hand and politely say, "Nice to meet you," while looking into the eyes of the person we would introduce to them. The adults they would meet would respond with praise and positive comments, and you could see the girls beam with pride. Good etiquette breeds compliments. Compliments breed self-confidence.

At age thirteen, I had my first job as a receptionist. I had to learn how to answer and operate the switchboard (yes, with the wire thingy) at my father's hotel directly across from the Montreal airport. Consequently, phone etiquette was important for me to teach my children. One morning, a gentleman called our home and Rachel, who was about five at the time, answered the phone. She said in her sweet little voice, "One moment please; please hold." Needless to say, my heart was bursting with pride when he asked me how old my daughter was.

Anne Platz and Susan Wales', *Social Graces: Manners, Conversations, and Charm for Today,* is a short reference book on etiquette that you may enjoy reading.

BOTTOM LINE — Etiquette is a prerequisite in nearly all aspects of life, both personal and professional. It should become second nature to your children as they grow up.

Note 10

Learning by Osmosis

Liza applied for a position at the Governor's office, as the assistant to the Director of External Affairs. It was her last year in college before going to law school. She could work full-time and complete her four remaining courses in the evenings.

One of the first questions they asked her was, "Have you ever planned any special events?" She replied, "Well, I worked with my mom when she organized events for two thousand people."

Liza is exceedingly capable. One year, at the last minute, we could not find anyone to take over the concession stands during intermission for one of our large events. I asked her if she would be willing to help, and she agreed and gathered a team from her school. She had the boys pick up the bottled water and sodas in their trucks. The girls got the crackers and cheese, muffins, cookies, and gourmet coffee. They set up and stocked all the booths, managed the cash boxes, and got everything done in a timely, orderly fashion.

Liza had learned how to organize concessions for such a large event by osmosis, as I like to call it. By being with her mama and helping out, she learned what it took to get things done. Over the years, both girls had the opportunity to work alongside me while I gave instructions to committee leaders and volunteers. As I would drag them around town, we would discuss problems and situations that came up and how to handle them correctly. These were invaluable learning experiences.

Involve your children in projects, big or small, as much as you are able. Explain the process while you are working. The more exposure, the more they will learn. This quote from poet and essayist Ralph Waldo Emerson illustrates this point perfectly: *"What you are speaks so loudly, I cannot hear what you say."*

BOTTOM LINE

You've heard the saying: "The apple doesn't fall far from the tree." Children become like their parents, because we are the first models they have to follow. So, my advice: Lead by example.

Teachers

In third grade, Rachel began the school year by coming home lamenting that she hated school. This was most unusual and a little troubling, since she always loved going to school.

She said that her teacher did not like her. I let it pass for a few days until one night, at bedtime, she told me how she was embarrassed when her teacher scolded her. Rachel always tried to please her teachers and didn't understand what she had done wrong.

I decided to ask for a meeting with the teacher and bring Rachel's Iowa test results from the earlier years. We chatted for a while, then I politely shared with her that Rachel believed her teacher did not like her. Using her Iowa Tests, I pointed out the area Rachel struggled with the most:

following directions. I explained to her that if she gave Rachel a task with multiple steps, she most likely would skip one of them. It was not because she was being defiant; she just forgot a part of the instructions.

Her teacher thanked me for sharing this information, and said she would keep this in mind in her class. That year became one of Rachel's favorite classes and she excelled in her studies. As Rachel read and edited this note, she described third grade as being a great year for her as the teacher took the time to repeat instructions for her, and from then on she stopped struggling in that area.

Rachel, who is now a teacher herself, says she appreciates when parents tell her about the areas her students struggle with and where they need extra help. It allows her to alter the way she interacts with each student to achieve the most success. However, there are times parents are unknowingly wrong when it comes to telling teachers how to do their job; it is wise not to judge their methods too quickly.

There are times we know better what is right for our child, and there are times we might be wrong.

One teacher required students to take copious notes and then rewrite them for homework following specific rules. Many students enjoyed and benefited from this teaching style and especially appreciated the love and respect this teacher had for his students. A few years later, a group of parents took it upon themselves to tell the principal rewriting notes was just "busy work" that added too much homework. They demanded to have the teacher stopped, and they won. It crushed the teacher's spirit to have this tried-and-true method questioned and forbidden in his classroom.

When Liza got to college, she recounted that this type of "busy work" was a tremendous help to her. She recognized the benefits as she established new study habits and made the transition to college. There is truth to the old saying, "There is a method to the madness." As far as I know, hard work is never a waste of time.

There are times we know better what is right for our child, and there are times we might be wrong. Always encourage teachers, and be courteous and respectful. Teach your child to do the same. Respecting authority and being courteous to adults is somewhat of a lost virtue these days.

BOTTOM LINE Share with your child's teacher if there is an area that he or she might struggle with, but do not be parents who constantly demand special treatment for their child.

Don't Rush Bedtime

Every night when the girls were young, I would hear Rachel call out to me when she would get into bed, "Mom, are you gonna come in?" She wanted me to lie in bed with her for a little while, maybe tell a story, say our prayers, and then chat.

Bedtime is the perfect time to get into our children's heads daily and find out what they are thinking about, what is going on in their lives, how they are feeling, or if they met new friends. It may be tempting to dismiss bedtime to enjoy a short uninterrupted moment alone. However, the more you engage your children in conversation, the more they will open up, which provides more opportunities to counsel your children on how to handle life's daily challenges.

By the time Rachel was in her mid-teens, she would only occasionally call me into her room. One night, after she was through talking, she turned to me and said, "Okay, you can go now." I replied, "No, I want to stay a little while longer." She started to push me off the bed with her feet as she giggled, "Mom, I like to sleep alone now, you should have taken advantage of it when I was little!" I fell off the bed laughing but with this bittersweet realization: that time in her life was over for me. Savor bedtime with your children! They will be grown before you know it, and you will have plenty of uninterrupted nights—much sooner than you think.

When you listen, really listen, to your children, it gives them a sense of security, stability, and a feeling of love.

Parents should make time to pay complete attention to what their children are saying. For instance, there were nights the girls would open up about personal issues, and I would just listen without giving advice or interrupting. I'd simply acknowledge what they were saying. This is called active listening, which is done by expressing encouraging words and using body language to show you are engaged in the conversation. It also is appropriate to restate or rephrase their words to ensure you understand what was said. After times like these, I'd go back to our room and tell my husband, "I would never have shared stuff like this with my mom!"

When you listen, *really listen*, to your children, it gives them a sense of security, stability, and a feeling of love. They are comfortable sharing intimate thoughts with you, because they do not fear ridicule or punishment. Later, you can go back to your kids with advice by starting with, "When you mentioned ____, did you think about ____?" Children will be more open to discuss issues and will share more information when their conversations are uninterrupted.

 A great book about talking and listening to children is *"How to Talk So Kids Will Listen & Listen So Kids Will Talk"* by Adele Faber and Elaine Mazlish. A must have in your library!

BOTTOM LINE

Keep an open line of communication (and an open mind) while children express their inner feelings. If not bedtime, find at least one time each day to have a special, quiet moment with each of your children to show them you are genuinely interested in what they have to say. Listen attentively. Don't criticize or try to fix their problems. Children need a sympathetic ear.

Note 13

Friends

The topic of friendships covers a lot of territory. Consequently, this note is the longest—and one of the most important—in the book. As children get older, for some, friendships become the center of their entire existence.

This was the case for both our girls. They continuously invited friends to our home. Maybe it was because we fed them no matter what time of day they came by, or simply because they knew we loved them. We literally had hundreds of young people pass through the Smokers' revolving door for birthday parties, student meetings, study groups, youth group meetings, movie nights, karaoke nights, school project nights, and any-excuse nights.

Sleepover birthday parties were my personal favorites. We would have as many as twenty girls setting up camp all over the living room floor and on the couches. When children spend the night at your home, you get to know them quickly, and vice versa! Which is a good thing, because the better they know you, the more respect they have for you and your children. And the less likely they will be to pull any "shenanigans."

My friend, Carla Hepp, let me in on her little sleepover secret: She set the clocks in her home ahead one hour so the girls thought they stayed up later. I improved on her stroke of genius by setting mine ahead two hours.

The fact our daughters and their friends felt so welcome in our home had its advantages: We always knew where they were, and that they were safe. That's what mattered most to my husband and me.

If plans changed when they were out, they would call to let us know. That was our agreement, and it may be the reason why we never needed to set a curfew. After a night out, they often would return with their friends to watch a movie. We much preferred to have them come back to our home instead of looking for a random place to hang out late in the evening.

Our home was also the designated spot for after-prom all-nighters. Our daughters and their friends would come back to our house dressed in their gowns and their suits for a midnight snack. They would stay up until dawn and would end the celebration by going to the beach to watch the sun rise.

You might think you can't afford to have an open house and entertain all your children's friends. I say, you can't afford not to. It's a lot cheaper to invest in a few bags of chips and deli meat than to pay for counseling sessions when you discover your child has been hanging out with the wrong crowds or is having serious issues with drugs or alcohol.

Here is another significant point for parents. "Don't be too quick to judge your children's friends." For many years, we had a monthly gathering for moms from Rachel's classroom. A new mom who just moved to the country saw a photo of our older daughter on the refrigerator and said, "My son should meet your daughter." The next month, she brought him to the meeting. As I opened the door, a young man wearing all black clothing with a dog collar style bracelet on his wrist and barrettes in his hair walked in. I thought to myself, "I don't think so!"

However, he turned out to be a most remarkable young man. His friendship to both our daughters was invaluable. He introduced his friends to the girls and it started a trend for the annual Prom Nights. The girls would find their friends a prom date by assigning one of his friends to one of theirs. Four years in a row, they went to proms together. We never worried because accompanying our girls and their friends were young men who would look out for them. Some were even expert social and ballroom dancers. It was an idyllic and fun time in their lives!

We had such a great relationship with the boys that my husband and I were invited to their weddings, and we still keep in touch today. As soon as they start their own family, you know they will be getting a signed copy of this booklet!

One of my fondest memories of a great role model was my best friend's mom. I cherished the way she made me feel valued as she welcomed me into her home. She became like a second mother, and I always will remember her. I am convinced she influenced the way I interacted with our children's friends.

Let me close with a word picture that my husband heard over the radio a very long time ago. Unfortunately, he did not get to hear who the speaker was, so I cannot credit authorship:

> *You are cooking in the kitchen one afternoon and the doorbell rings. You go to the door and a little child at your doorstep asks you if he could come in and eat*

dinner with your family and if he could stay overnight. You would probably start looking around as you wondered whom this child belongs to and maybe even call the police.

On the other hand, if your own child walked in from school while you were cooking in the kitchen, and called out that their friend is staying for dinner and would be sleeping over so they could study for a big test, you would probably continue your work in the kitchen and say, "Okay!"

Picture the same scene in heaven. Only this time, Jesus is walking into his Father's home, and you are walking in behind him. God looks at you and then looks at his son. Jesus smiles at Him and says, "He's with me."

That is a beautiful picture of our first meeting with God, and I imagine He will greet us with a warm welcome just as my best friend's mom did when I followed him into his house.

BOTTOM LINE

Get to know your children's friends by continuously having them over to your house. Don't judge them by their outward appearance; instead take time to get to know them.

Dollars and Sense

We started early teaching our girls about money: how to spend it and how to save it. Our first step was to create a list of chores, in addition to their daily responsibilities, that the girls could complete to earn extra money. For example, if they cleaned the bathroom sinks, they would get a quarter. If they matched socks from the clean laundry, they would get a nickel for each pair of socks they matched. For larger amounts of money, they could vacuum a room, rake leaves, etc. When it was time to go to the store, the girls would ask how many sinks they needed to clean to afford a certain toy. These paid chores helped them understand how more expensive items required more work.

We applied a similar concept during family vacations: We gave the girls a gift of money to spend, but emphasized this was all they would receive for the duration of the trip. It was interesting to watch them check the price of each item and evaluate just how much they wanted it. Frequently, they decided to purchase the one on sale and put the more expensive one back. They knew once their allowance was depleted, there was no more cash coming.

This approach educates children on how to manage their money, which reduces whining and begging and lays a foundation for a healthy relationship with money. It also teaches the value of comparison vs. impulse shopping, saving for large-ticket items, and living within a budget.

Children always will have "wants" that parents may not be able to afford. It is okay to say, "I don't have the money to buy this now," or "I wish I had a magic wand so I could make it appear for you." Show empathy for their wishes, but do not give them everything they ask for. The earlier they learn life's real lessons, the better handle they will have dealing with their own finances.

The earlier they learn life's real lessons, the better handle they will have dealing with their own finances.

For instance, we provided our girls with basic clothing, school items, and whatever they needed. If they wanted extra-special items or a designer brand, we were totally fine with that; however, they had to pay the difference from their own hard-earned money. This helped the girls learn to make wise spending choices.

As they got older, we applied this same approach to larger financial decisions. Since my husband and I both had to pay for our own college education, we told the girls we would help them by paying half of their college expenses. When Liza was in middle school, we overheard her say, "I have to get good grades so I can get full scholarships, because I have to pay for half my college." Inadvertently, it motivated our girls to be better students and better stewards of their money. They saved the money they made from babysitting or cleaning offices and any gift money they received into the bank accounts we set up for them when they were born.

When our girls graduated from high school, they both received full scholarships; we still paid the half we promised. They were able to attend college without having to work. They invested their time studying to ensure they got good grades so they could keep their scholarships.

When it came time to purchase cars, we told them we would buy them any car they wanted; they just had to pay for half of it. The girls waited until their sophomore year of college before shopping for their first cars. Their father taught them the ins and outs of choosing and how to haggle for the best deal available. They were thrilled when the day finally came to drive their own wheels and not mom's brown, high-top minivan that could have doubled for a UPS truck.

 I believe one of the best and most successful programs about finance is: *Financial Peace University by* Dave Ramsey. It is recommended not only for high school and college students but adults of all ages. You learn to take control of your money, invest for the future and give like never before. For more information, visit www.daveramsey.com.

BOTTOM LINE Develop your own system to teach your children about money. Just be sure to start when they are very young. Show compassion for their wishes, but you do not need to give them everything they want. When they are older, they will understand the value of a dollar and live within their means, which is one of the most valuable gifts you could ever give them.

The Penalty Box

Allow me to share a story (just to embarrass myself). In 1997, we were invited to attend a Marlins' game during the World Series. My husband told me to get a couple of Marlins' shirts. I went to the store and told the young man who was helping me that I was going to the World Series with friends who had box seats! While he was showing me different shirts, I said, "Do you mind if I ask you a question? The Marlins: are they a football team or a baseball team?" He retorted, "Lady, you don't deserve to go to the World Series!" Fortunately, I have learned a bit more about sports since that day!

I was born in Canada where hockey is a big deal. My older brother watched the games every Saturday night. No matter where we were in the house, we would know when the Canadians scored by his loud cheers. My favorite part of the game was when all the gloves flew across the skating rink and a fight would break out. Then, there was the penalty box routine.

The penalized player walked like a mad gorilla on skates and jumped into the penalty box. The game kept running without any attention to him, until the clock struck ten seconds. Then everyone would start the countdown, "10, 9, 8, 7, 6, 5, 4, 3, 2, 1!" The crowd would cheer wildly as the player came out of the penalty box and re-emerged onto the skating rink, yielding through the players, right back into the game!

We heard Dr. J. Zink using the penalty box metaphor while speaking on children and discipline. He equipped parents for a lifetime with simple methods that both mom and dad could agree on and were easy to implement. He suggested to come up with five short rules that would apply to each individual family unit: rules that would make for a better life for everyone in the household. For each rule that was broken, assign an appropriate and fair consequence.

"The penalty box" was one of several consequences suggested for breaking a rule. He recommended the most boring room in the house, perhaps a chair in the dining room, where the child must sit quietly until the timer rings. Just like hockey, as the timer approached the 10-second mark, you, the parent, can start the countdown and high five your child for doing a great job sitting quietly in the penalty box.

Some rule-breaking infringements require more serious consequences as children grow older such as going to bed a half hour earlier, losing car privileges, or being grounded.

Children know the rules and need to learn to follow them. By presetting the rules—and the consequences—you will have more peace: no embarrassment, no nagging!

Our family took it one-step further. When we were out in public, we came up with the code words: "Why are we good?" If we had to say it twice, the girls would expect a consequence when they got home. Using this method, we did not scold or embarrass them in front of people, and they appreciated that (and so did the other people).

Explain the behavior you expect and the consequences when rules are broken. That way, everyone knows where everyone stands. It is absolutely critical to be consistent.

Countless authors have written books on the basic premise of discipline: all choices have consequences. For a list of book recommendations, check the back of this booklet.

 Take a moment to browse through the Center for Transformative Teacher Training on the Web. I was introduced to the teaching of Lee Canter through his books *Assertive Discipline, A Take-Charge Approach for Today's Educators and Assertive Discipline for Parents.* I found his methods extremely helpful.

BOTTOM LINE According to experts in the field of child discipline, a positive approach for youngsters is to "catch them being good" and let them know you did. When they mess up (and they will), there is no need to scream or get upset. Just as the referee simply blows the whistle in hockey, calmly state the consequence as the result of their wrong choice or action, then follow through!

Note 16

Every Day is a Choice

When the girls were toddlers, I got to a place where I was extremely exhausted and depressed. Having moved away from my family, I no longer had my parents, siblings, and other close family and friends nearby for support. As my stress and my energy waned, I felt overwhelmed and was losing patience with my two precious daughters.

One time I screamed so loud that Liza, who was three years old, put her arms up in the air and said, "Mom, I think I'm in the wrong house!" I realized that I needed to adjust my attitude. Whether screaming is a learned behavior or a habit, losing control produces fear and anxiety, and is very detrimental to children.

Parenthood can be stressful—or should I say parenthood is very stressful at times! However, there is a light at the end of the tunnel. Once we understand that the stress is universal, we can take a deep breath and look for new strategies. When I share with parents embarrassing moments, struggles, and mistakes I made as a mom, I can see their body language shift and their facial expressions relax as they realize they are not alone.

Another life-changing moment was when I attended the funeral of my friend's child. Before the service started, I began crying to the point of suffocation, the pain was so great. From that moment forward, I completely reprioritized my life as a parent. It was a cosmic thump on the head—one that filled me with gratitude for my family and taught me the importance of focusing on the bigger picture.

A good place to start altering your outlook is by changing your perspective. You may have heard the saying "every day is a choice"—you choose your attitude, and you decide how you will respond to things throughout your day. If you do not know where to start, create a perpetual list of everything you are thankful for: anything from your ability to see and walk, to your family, and your health. Review it daily and continue to add to it as you think of new things.

Take time to stop and enjoy the world around you. Go outdoors and revel in life's simple pleasures: sunrises, sunsets, birds, flowers, anything that brings you joy. Encourage your family to join you. Have them make their own lists. Be a family that looks for and recognizes the good in every situation. When you center your attention on the positive and fill your mind with happy thoughts, it leaves little room for grumbling and negativity.

 Pat Holt and Grace Ketterman, M.D., *When you feel like Screaming! Help for Frustrated Mothers*. Harold Shaw Publishers, 1988.

BOTTOM LINE Stress during parenting is universal. Change your thought process and show the love! Focus on the good things in people. Choose to be an encourager instead of a critic. Choose to be happy rather than grumpy. *Fix your mind on what is true, what is right, what is pure, and what is admirable.*

THIS IS YOUR LIFE.
DO WHAT YOU LOVE, AND DO IT OFTEN.
IF YOU DON'T LIKE SOMETHING, CHANGE IT.
IF YOU DON'T LIKE YOUR JOB, QUIT.
IF YOU DON'T HAVE ENOUGH TIME, STOP WATCHING TV.
IF YOU ARE LOOKING FOR THE LOVE OF YOUR LIFE, STOP;
THEY WILL BE WAITING FOR YOU WHEN YOU
START DOING THINGS YOU LOVE.
STOP OVER ANALYZING, ALL EMOTIONS ARE BEAUTIFUL.
LIFE IS SIMPLE. WHEN YOU EAT, APPRECIATE EVERY LAST BITE.
OPEN YOUR MIND, ARMS, AND HEART TO NEW THINGS
AND PEOPLE, WE ARE UNITED IN OUR DIFFERENCES.
ASK THE NEXT PERSON YOU SEE WHAT THEIR PASSION IS,
AND SHARE YOUR INSPIRING DREAM WITH THEM.
TRAVEL OFTEN; GETTING LOST WILL HELP YOU FIND YOURSELF.
SOME OPPORTUNITIES ONLY COME ONCE, SEIZE THEM.
LIFE IS ABOUT THE PEOPLE YOU MEET, AND
THE THINGS YOU CREATE WITH THEM
SO GO OUT AND START CREATING.
LIFE IS LIVE YOUR DREAM,
SHORT. AND WEAR YOUR PASSION.

With permission from "The Holstee Manifesto" © 2009, holstee.com Design by Rachael Beresh.

Note 17

Looking Ahead

Here are a few excerpts from my journal around the time both of my girls left for college. It may fast-forward you to what you might experience when you finally have to let your children go.

August 18, 2004

So, here I am, the eve before our girls leave for college together for the first time. My heart is broken. How many times did I have to redo my make-up this past week because I cried at the thought of them leaving? How foolish did I look when I paid the cashier, telling her the fruit was for my daughters' trip to college in the morning, and what a sad day it was going to be, as tears began to stream down my cheeks.

Where have the years gone? They were so little just a bit ago. I'm going to miss them so much. The thoughts going through my head are too painful to write, but I know what they are.

Regrets... yes, many. Yet they are both so precious regardless of my mistakes and my shortcomings. "God watch over them yourself; don't just send your angels. Please stay close to them and bless them."

August 19, 2004

I stayed up until two in the morning last night. I was in the den and had to use a face cloth to wipe my face drowning in tears. My eyes were swollen, and I could not stop sobbing. At five a.m., I woke up well before the girls got up and put on a full face of make-up to hide my pain. I did okay, until I was running next to the car waving to them both. Liza turned and looked me straight in my eyes. I smiled at her as my eyes filled up with tears, and then I stopped running, letting them go. I stood in the middle of our street and watched them until they drove out of sight. I walked back into the house with such a heavy heart. I entered the kitchen, sobbing uncontrollably, and said to my husband, "This is the day I was dreading all my life."

August 23, 2004

A few days later, a hurricane hit us, and we have no power. I found myself standing in the hallway by the girls' rooms with a lantern in my hand. I stood in the darkness and looked into their rooms. It was so quiet and still perfectly clean. It was the end of a season. I wish I had stayed a little longer with them and had told them more bedtime stories. I wish I had looked into their eyes more often when they told me about their days when I lay next to them in bed. How I wish I could go back in time and hold my babies in my arms again.

We know our children grow up fast. We see it happen before our eyes, but I don't think we can realize how short time is until the day they are gone. When it happens, some of us feel like we were hit by a brick. You become anxious thinking you had lots more to give, but it's too late. You can't turn back time.

 A book that may inspire you to start journaling:
Nicole Johnson, *Fresh-Brewed Life, A Stiring Invitation to Wake Up Your Soul*, Thomas Nelson Publisher, 1999.

BOTTOM LINE With child rearing, there is no remote control with a "pause" or "rewind" button. Do what you can while you have them. Nothing compares with the satisfaction of knowing that you have done your best.

Note 18

The Clean Slate Method

In the early nineties, I read a book that included a list of thirty emotional needs people need to receive during their childhood in order to be "whole." After going over the list, I decided I was not going to miss the mark as a mom. I invited the girls, who were about nine and eleven years old, into the kitchen to sit at the table. We went over the thirty needs one by one. To say their opinions were eye opening is an understatement.

For each emotional need, they would answer, as indicated in the book, if they received it from me, their dad, both of us or neither of us. When there was one need that was not quite met, they would say things like, "but at least when you get upset with us, you don't stay upset long, and we know it's over. But with dad," they said laughing, "we have to listen to long, long lectures, and that is worse."

This emotional needs exercise afforded me an opportunity to apologize for the times I had messed up and for the emotional needs I had not truly succeeded in fulfilling for my girls. Asking for forgiveness for my mistakes was something I did with them from a young age.

It reminds me of an evening when I was tucking Liza in bed. She was sucking her thumb looking at me as I told her I was sorry for screaming at her that day. I hugged her and she patted me on the back with her small hand, took her thumb out of her mouth and said, "It's okay mommy, I forgive you."

BOTTOM LINE

Apologize when you mess up. It is vital for parents to admit to their children when they are wrong. Most important, parents must ask them for forgiveness. I call it the "clean slate" method. It is important to deal with problems as soon as they occur so everyone can move forward with nothing left unsettled.

Here is the list of the thirty emotional needs:

1. Acceptance
2. Admonition
3. Affection
4. Appreciation
5. Approval
6. Attention
7. Comfort
8. Compassion
9. Confession
10. Deference
11. Devotion
12. Discipline
13. Edification
14. Encouragement
15. Forgiveness
16. Harmony
17. Hospitality
18. Intimacy
19. Kindness
20. Love
21. Prayer
22. Respect
23. Security
24. Serving
25. Support
26. Sympathy
27. Teaching
28. Tolerance
29. Training
30. Understanding

Taken from *"Intimate Encounters,"* By Dr. David and Teresa Ferguson, GreatCommandment.net, 2511 South Lakeline Blvd., Cedar Park, Texas 78613. (Used with permission.)

Note 19

Character Traits

Larry King shared this funny story on his program: He visited a relative with his wife in a nursing home. There was a group of elderly people sitting in the lobby as he walked in. An elderly man, hunched over in a chair, slightly lifted his head and said, "Larry King, big deal." Larry King was laughing recalling the moment, recognizing that we all reach a point in life where what seemed important may no longer matter, and the little things in life will matter a great deal.

When my mom entered the first stages of Alzheimer's, my parents had to move from their home to an independent living center. One morning, as I was returning to my parent's apartment, a tiny, older woman came out at the other end of the hallway and waited for the elevator. When the doors opened, she said, "There is no one in the elevator; I'm alone. I'm always alone." It really struck a chord in my heart.

Seniors often vocalize what they are thinking. Like children, they have no social filter. We get to hear what is in their hearts and on their minds. The world would be a more caring place if we could see or hear people's innermost feelings.

You may have seen the Liberty Mutual commercial on television. It begins with one person picking up a toy for a baby in a stroller while another is watching. Next scene, that person helps another, while a third person watches and so it goes. This one act of kindness becomes contagious—*a trickledown effect of goodness!*

Parents should want their children to grow up to be compassionate, kind, honest, generous, loving, respectful, loyal, helpful, caring and trustworthy individuals. But wanting doesn't make it so. These traits are taught by example and by practice.

The girls and I practiced kindness and charity as we did unique and unexpected things for people. One time, we were shopping at a Good Will Center and noticed a sweet family with little children shopping for household items. When they got to the cash register, we walked by, handed them a $20 bill, said, "God bless your family," and left the store. It gave us the idea for Christmas time, to put money in envelopes and randomly hand them out to people in need.

Another day, we were at the grocery store and it was apparent that the elderly woman behind us had walked a long distance to the store with a cart on wheels and she was red from the sun. We handed $15 to the cashier and told her to use it for part of this woman's groceries after we left. The cashier was excited and grateful that she would be part of this blessing. You get an amazing feeling from doing little acts of love to strangers in need. But I can't take credit for this. I learned it from my dad.

While on vacation one year, my dad was treating us to ice cream when a woman walked in and asked for a glass of water. The attendant handed her a tiny condiment cup filled with water. Dad ordered and paid for a large drink and asked the clerk to hand it to the woman. That left quite an impression on me, and I shared this lesson with my children. Now, when they are driving by homeless people, they often hand out water bottles and a pack of peanut-butter crackers and they help feed the hungry in different programs as well as volunteer in different charitable organizations.

Another characteristic my dad valued highly was a strong work ethic. He owned several businesses, and taught us the value of a good employee every chance he had.

My mom hired a neighbor to help her with the ironing. When the clock struck noon, Mrs. Tremblay unplugged the iron and left for lunch before finishing the skirt she was ironing. My dad came home and looked over at the ironing board. He pointed out that instead of taking an extra minute to finish the job, she had left the skirt half-ironed because it was time for lunch. He explained employers notice when their employees do the bare minimum and that they are not the ones chosen when promotion time rolls around.

My father also had a strong sense of fairness and honesty. Did you ever tell a cashier that she or he gave you too much change back? My dad always did. And he never got over how they were always surprised. He thought that was a sad commentary on people's expectations.

I laugh when I think of the day my daughters and I went to a drive-thru restaurant. We found an extra sandwich in the bag, which we were not charged for, and the girls insisted that I turn back and return it. Since we were running late for a rehearsal I promised we would go back the next day and pay for it. The next day, we did just that. We went back and told one of the cashiers we had to pay for an extra sandwich they gave us by mistake. The girls felt good about it, and I was super proud of their determination to be honest even in the little things, especially when no one would have known.

BOTTOM LINE Teach your children to be respectful, caring, honest and hard-working individuals. Employers know that dedicated employees are hard to find. You would do your child a great service to foster these qualities in their character with an extra dose of going beyond what is required or expected— going the second mile. Remember, character is doing the right thing when nobody is watching.

Note 20

School Notes

As parents, we are our children's first educators. It is up to us to set good learning habits through structure and daily routines and to provide the best environment for their brain development.

We read books to our children every night while standing next to their crib. Reading to children provides the important educational benefits that guarantee success in your child's education. Studies prove that even at this early age, reading improves literacy development and prepares children for future academic achievements.

We surrounded our children with books. Each month, we would visit the library and get dozens of books. When we arrived home, we would place the baby books on the bottom shelf for Rachel who was still crawling. Liza's books found a home on the second bottom shelf. Everywhere we went, we took books along. Whenever we waited for appointments, we read. Before bed, we read. Books were a huge part of our lives.

Both girls were straight A students throughout their school years, not because they were smarter than others, but because they worked hard at their studies. We made sure they knew from Day 1, that their job was to do their best in their studies because it would set their whole future in motion. They were responsible to get their homework done on time, and we were there to help them study. We taught them fun memory techniques when they struggled with math and spelling.

Some parents' first approach to bad grades is punishment. They ground their child to show their disapproval. A more constructive approach is to tell your child you will help him or her with challenging subject matter by engaging a tutor or finding a friend or study group to help.

Too many precious family moments are lost forever with the technology phenomenon that has hoodwinked our culture into believing we need to stay constantly connected.

Just as we did not allow television on school nights, if I were a parent of young children today, I definitely would limit time spent on iPads, iPhones and other high-tech devices as well. Too many precious family moments are lost forever with the technology phenomenon that has hoodwinked our culture into believing we need to stay constantly connected.

 Jack Lannon, Memory Genius® *The Secret of Maximum Mental Performance*© Lannom Incorporated

BOTTOM LINE Read without ceasing to your children. It will improve literacy development and prepare them for future academic achievements. Train your children to become responsible for their schoolwork by helping them set good study habits early on and by teaching them how to learn through different methods and memory techniques.

Note 21

Leaving a Legacy

This booklet is dedicated to my father and my mother who passed away in 2011 and 2009 respectively.

They raised the six of us in the faith. I always joked with my older brother, who is a priest, that he was their favorite. (He does not like it when I say that). We were all favorites in their eyes even though I was called the black sheep of the family at times. Although I did not have a great relationship with my father as I grew up, I cherish his words of wisdom, his teaching and his guidance—all of which are reflected in this booklet. While both parents passed on a legacy rich in love and wisdom I am most thankful for their gift of prayer and of faith.

In 1982, I was told that I would probably have problems having children. I came home from the doctor's office, sat on the couch totally depressed. I shared this with my husband. He simply said, "Put it in God's hands, and forget about it." I shrugged my shoulders and said, "Okay." The next month, I was pregnant with our first-born, Liza.

When I was in seventh grade, one morning, on the busy corner by our home, I started to cross the street when the light turned green. A white car pulled around a stopped bus. In slow motion, I watched as the car came full speed right at me. I do not recall how, but suddenly I was safely back on the sidewalk.

Meanwhile, my dad was in his bedroom reading a letter from a nun from another country. It said, "We are praying for you. Perhaps God has already bestowed a blessing to your family." At that very moment, he heard a loud screeching of brakes. He ran out the front door, as I was running back up the steps of our duplex, shaking and white as a sheet.

I believe that sometimes coincidences are indeed God-incidences. I have seen miracles in my life and in the lives of my children. When Liza was three years old, we told her we were going to move because our house was getting too small for all four of us. Liza began to pray at night, "Dear Lord, I would like to have a pink room with pink furniture." She repeatedly prayed this prayer. One day, I told her, "There's no such thing as pink furniture, Liza, I've never seen any."

A few years later, I took Liza with me to check out a home my husband had seen for sale. Before we arrived, I asked God to give me a sign if this was to be our new home. We walked through the house, the kitchen, the garage, out into the backyard, then back into the house to the last bedroom. Lo and behold, there was a pink room with pink furniture! Liza ran into the bedroom, stood next to the bed and said, "Mommy, mommy, is this my room, is this our house?"

After a few months in our new home, we had a large tree on the front lawn cut down. My husband and I were standing by the driveway cleaning up the yard when a young man came by with a brand new stump grinder and asked if he could try it out on our trunk at no charge. We looked at each other in disbelief. How in the world would someone walk by our house with a brand spanking new stump grinder on the very day we had our tree cut?

I have dozens of stories like these. All I know is that prayers are answered, and miracles happen. I truly believe that having a mom and dad who prayed for us made a difference in our lives.

I believe that sometimes coincidences are indeed God-incidences.

If you come from a family that may not have bestowed the legacy of prayer on you, why not be the first in your family and change the course for your children, grandchildren and great grandchildren?

Twice a year Dr. Bob Barnes spoke to our mothers' group. One day he shared this word picture: he said that when we die, God will show us what our lives would have been like had we spent time in prayer with Him. It was as if someone had stamped that image on my forehead with a hot iron. I never forgot it!

 Robert G. Barnes Jr., Ph.D., has written several books on parenting including *Who's in Charge Here?* and *Raising Confident Kids.* Dr. Barnes continues to do much for the community of South Florida. You will find more information at www.parentingonpurpose.org.

BOTTOM LINE

We use prayers and vigils to show support during a crisis in the world and when dealing with a tragic illness or death. When prayers are answered, our faith is strengthened. Imagine what prayer can do in your family. Believe it, and watch God in action in your life!

A Last Word

Thank you for caring enough about children to read this book in its entirety. Parents, like you, who are seeking to be the best parents they can be, will change future generations for the better!

I was never able to cover all the information in our parenting sessions. So, I developed handouts to capture what was missed. Got Kids? Take Notes! is the result of parents encouraging me to turn my musings into a booklet.

We encourage you to read a book or two on parenting every year or attend a parenting conference or seminar. Keeping current helps refresh your outlook and gives you insight into setting new goals as your children are growing up. You will find a list of book recommendations on parenting at the end of this book.

I would love to hear from you. Please feel free to write and share a story of your own. We might even post it on our website!

Got Kids? Take Notes!
P.O. Box 4592
Fort Lauderdale, FL 33338
GotKidsTakeNotes.com

If I Had a Second Chance

Two of my favorite family movies are "The Kid" with Bruce Willis, and "Hook" with Robin Williams. I love, love, love these movies! Have a family movie night and enjoy these if you haven't already. In both movies, the main characters are given a second chance at life. Here is what I would do differently as a mom if I had a second chance.

• I would stop moving so fast. I would focus less on crossing items off my daily to-do list, and think more along the lines of "Why do today what you can do tomorrow."

• I would wait to clean and organize the house until after the children left for college :o). It would give me the freedom to enjoy life more, and I would fret less.

• I would welcome interruptions from my children and cherish the fact that they come to us when they need something, because we are the most important persons in their lives.

• I would kneel down at these interruptions, look into my toddler's eyes and listen more attentively. I'd drink in their precious baby features as they chat away.

• I would spend more time sitting on the floor and playing with my children.

• I would brag about them more often when they were within hearing range to build their self-esteem even more.

"Things Moms Say"
Author unknown

The following "mom-isms" have been circulating on the Web. They're guaranteed to make you LOL!

1. My mother taught me TO APPRECIATE A JOB WELL DONE.
   "If you're going to kill each other, do it outside. I just finished cleaning."

2. My mother taught me RELIGION.
   "You better pray that that spill will come out of the carpet."

3. My mother taught me about TIME TRAVEL.
   "If you don't straighten up, I'm going to knock you into the middle of next week!"

4. My mother taught me LOGIC.
   "Because I said so, that's why."

5. My mother taught me MORE LOGIC.
   "If you fall out of that swing and break your neck, you're not going to the store with me."

6. My mother taught me FORESIGHT.
   "Make sure you wear clean underwear, in case you're in an accident."

7. My mother taught me IRONY.
   "Keep crying and I'll give you something to cry about."

8. My mother taught me about the science of OSMOSIS.
   "Shut your mouth and eat your supper."

9. My mother taught me about CONTORTIONISM.
   "Will you look at that dirt on the back of your neck?"

10. My mother taught me about STAMINA.
    "You'll sit there until all that spinach is gone."

11. My mother taught me about WEATHER.
    "This room of yours looks as if a tornado went through it."

12. My mother taught me about HYPOCRISY.
    "If I told you once, I've told you a million times. Don't exaggerate!"
13. My mother taught me the CIRCLE OF LIFE.
    "I brought you into this world, and I can take you out..."
14. My mother taught me about BEHAVIOR MODIFICATION.
    "Stop acting like your father!"
15. My mother taught me about ENVY.
    "There are millions of less fortunate children in this world who don't have wonderful parents like you do."
16. My mother taught me about ANTICIPATION.
    "Just wait until we get home."
17. My mother taught me about RECEIVING.
    "You are going to get it when your father gets home!"
18. My mother taught me MEDICAL SCIENCE.
    "If you don't stop crossing your eyes, they are going to get stuck that way."
19. My mother taught me ESP.
    "Put your sweater on; don't you think I know when you are cold?"
20. My mother taught me HUMOR.
    "When that lawn mower cuts off your toes, don't come running to me."
21. My mother taught me HOW TO BECOME AN ADULT.
    "If you don't eat your vegetables, you'll never grow up."
22. My mother taught me GENETICS.
    "You're just like your father."
23. My mother taught me about my ROOTS.
    "Shut that door behind you. Do you think you were born in a barn?"
24. My mother taught me WISDOM.
    "When you get to be my age, you'll understand."
25. My mother taught me about JUSTICE.
    "One day you'll have kids, and I hope they turn out just like you!"

Recommended Resources

Lee Canter with Marlene Canter, *Assertive Discipline for Parents* (Harper & Row, 1982)

Foster Cline, M.D. & Jim Fay, *Parenting With Love and Logic, Teaching Children Responsibility* (Pinon Press, 1990)

Dr. Henry Cloud and Dr. Jon Townsend, *Boundaries with Kids* (Zondervan, 1998)

Adele Faber & Elaine Mazlish, *How To Talk So Kids Will Listen &Listen So Kids Will Talk* (Scribner, 1980)

Mary Hunt, *The Complete Cheapskate* (Broadman & Holman, 1998)

Nicole Johnson, *Fresh Brewed Life* (Nelson Publishing, 1999)

Laurie Beth Jones, *The Path Creating Your Mission Statement* (Hyperion, 1996)

Jack Lannon, Memory Genius® *The Secret of Maximum Mental Performance*"© Lannom Incorporated

Ann Platz and Susan Wales, *Social Graces Manners, Conversation and Charm for Today* (Harvest House Publishers, 1998)

Dave Ramsey, *Financial Peace University*, daveramsey.com

Carol Simontacchi, *Crazy Makers, How the Food Industry Is Destroying Our Brains and Harming Our Children* (Tarcher Putnam Books, 2000)

Cynthia Ulrich Tobias, *You Can't Make Me* (WaterBrook Press 1999)

Susan Alexander Yates, *And Then I Had Kids* (Wolgemuth &Hyatt Publishers, Inc)

Zig Ziglar, *Raising Positive Kids in a Negative World*, (Oliver-Nelson Books, 1985)

Dr. J. Zink,Ph.D, *Upbringing*, (The Perengrinzilla Press, 1997)